...ed
...ds,
...el.

For more than 135 years our
guidebooks have ...ed the secrets
...he world,
...vealth of
...or travel.

...: as your
...next trip
...heritage.

Thomas Cook **pocket** guides

YORK

Your travelling companion since 1873

Written by David Cawley

Published by Thomas Cook Publishing
A division of Thomas Cook Tour Operations Limited
Company registration no. 3772199 England
The Thomas Cook Business Park, Unit 9, Coningsby Road,
Peterborough PE3 8SB, United Kingdom
Email: books@thomascook.com, Tel: +44 (0) 1733 416477
www.thomascookpublishing.com

Produced by Cambridge Publishing Management Limited
Burr Elm Court, Main Street, Caldecote CB23 7NU
www.cambridgepm.co.uk

ISBN: 978-1-84848-471-9

This first edition © 2011 Thomas Cook Publishing
Text © Thomas Cook Publishing
Cartography supplied by Redmoor Design, Tavistock, Devon
Map data © OpenStreetMap contributors CC-BY-SA,
www.openstreetmap.org, www.creativecommons.org

Series Editor: Karen Beaulah
Production/DTP: Steven Collins

Printed and bound in Spain by GraphyCems

Cover photography © Thomas Cook Publishing

CONTENTS

SYMBOLS KEY

The following symbols are used throughout this book:

ⓐ address **ⓣ** telephone **ⓦ** website address **ⓔ** email
ⓛ opening times **ⓝ** public transport connections **ⓘ** important

The following symbols are used on the maps:

𝒊 information office		**✉**	post office
✈ airport		▣	POI (point of interest)
✚ hospital		O	city
⬚ police station		O	large town
▤ bus station		○	small town
▤ railway station		—	main road
✝ church			minor road
▣ shopping		—	railway
❶ numbers denote featured cafés, restaurants & venues			

PRICE CATEGORIES

The ratings below indicate average price rates for a double room per night, including breakfast:

£ under £70 ££ £70–150 £££ over £150

The typical cost for a three-course meal without drinks is as follows:

£ under £20 ££ £20–30 £££ over £30

◍ *York Minster*

INTRODUCING
York

Introduction

Small in stature, colossal in its multitude of treasures, York is a remarkably beautiful and compelling city that has been capturing the hearts of visitors for the past two millennia. Whatever the reasons for coming here, visitors will find a fantastically compact city globally famous for its multiple layers of well-preserved history set among a labyrinthine tangle of medieval streets. Dominated by the vast, soaring edifice of York Minster, the city centre is steeped in a winning and balanced mix of history, culture and charm, carefully infused with style and infectious *joie de vivre*. With 30 museums and galleries alone, sightseeing can be almost overwhelming for the first-time visitor, as the city presents a vast array of things to do and see.

For those less engaged with history, York offers wonderful riverside walking, some excellent street theatre and some of the best and most unique shopping opportunities in the UK, continually attracting every age, taste and budget. It's certainly not all chintz tea shops, genteel boutiques and intense history lessons. With a population of fewer than 200,000, York's inhabitants also live in a smart, sophisticated city, while – once the sun goes down – two universities and a collection of colleges help create a fun and lively atmosphere. In the evening its narrow cobbled streets repopulate with throngs of gourmands, culture-seekers and all-round revellers, out to make the most of all that the city has to offer them. And there's plenty: restaurants, concert, theatre and cinema venues, countless chic bars and traditional pubs.

If sightseeing, shopping and busy city street life all get a little too much, the rustic freedom and solitude of some of Britain's finest remote moorland, tranquil villages and a varied coastal display of beaches, coves, resorts and quaint harbour towns are just a short journey away in the North York Moors.

For one so small, the city is crammed to its encircling walls with mesmerising splendour and heritage, where the old encompasses the new and where the unexpected can be found around every street corner.

⬥ *A stunning view from the Minster*

When to go

SEASONS & CLIMATE

York is a busy year-round destination, but as with all other British cities, spring and summer are the most pleasant, if not the busiest, times to be there, especially for those who simply like to amble and browse, or anyone in search of some outdoor pursuits in the nearby countryside.

Average temperatures jump from 1°C (34°F) in January and February to 21°C (70°F) in July and August but, given this is Britain, even at the height of summer rain is possible, and an umbrella can be a wise accessory.

ANNUAL EVENTS

With an abundance of cultural, historic and retail events there is almost certain to be something going on in the city whatever the time of year. The **Jorvik Viking Festival** offers a bumper celebration of all things Norse with appeal for young and old through **February** (ⓦ www.jorvik-viking-centre.co.uk), while lovers of the spoken and written word should enjoy ten days of literary celebration during **The York Literature Festival** (ⓦ www.yorkliteraturefestival.co.uk) in **March**. Stepping back in time again, **May** sees the **York Roman Festival** entertain and educate visiting families with all kinds of interactive fun and displays (ⓦ www.yorkromanfestival.org.uk). The internationally acclaimed **York Early Music Festival** (ⓐ St Margaret's Church, Percy's Lane ⓣ 01904 658338 ⓦ www.ncem.co.uk) takes place in both **July** and **December**, with a programme of concerts, workshops and talks featuring music from the Middle Ages onwards. Riverside and water fun comes with the **Festival of the Rivers** in **July**, when all manner of aquatic themed races and events take place on the Ouse River and its tributary, the Foss.

Also in **July** and first performed in the early 14th century, the **York Mystery Plays**, one of the oldest drama cycles in England, takes place every four years throughout the month, recounting the Bible from Creation to the Last Judgement in a series of public street performances (ⓦ www.yorkmysteryplays.co.uk). From early **November** thoughts are already turning towards Christmas with the cobbled streets transforming into a wonderland composed of ice sculptures, market stalls (including the **St Nicholas Market Fayre**), street entertainment, an open-air ice rink (ⓦ www.theicefactor.co.uk) and guaranteed 'snow'. The celebrations all culminate in the **Festival of Angels** in **mid-December** (ⓦ www.yorkfestivals.com).

🔺 *There's always some entertainment to be found in the streets of York*

History

George VI (1895–1952) has been quoted as saying, York is 'the history of England'. Indeed, the city can be seen as an anthology of the country's history, tracing its abundantly preserved lineage from the Bronze Age period through the Romans, Saxons, Vikings, Normans, Plantagenets, Tudors, Stuarts and Victorians.

In AD 71, York's rise to power as the capital of Lower Britain began in earnest when the Romans – at the height of their imperial power – conquered the Celtic Brigantes tribe and created the fort and town of Eboracum over the area now

🔺 *The Railway Museum illustrates how the industry charged the city*

surrounding the Minster. With the fort disbanded and the Romans gone, the town became known by resident Saxons as Eoferwic, until the Vikings arrived by longship up the River Ouse during the 9th century, establishing 'Jorvik' as a principal trading centre. This was one of the bloodiest periods in the city's long history; Eric Bloodaxe became King of York in 940, arriving with a reputation of having already killed seven of his eight brothers.

The Minster and existing stone walls, which are still in superb condition, were constructed by invading Normans from the 11th century onwards. Kings and queens were to become regular visitors, and the dukedom of York began to be conferred on the reigning sovereign's second son – as it still is today. This was also the period when medieval York was to regain its former Roman status and become the second largest and most important city in England, driven by an economy run by over a hundred different craft and trade guilds, several of whose halls can still be visited.

From the 18th century onwards, commerce and industry were to feature strongly in the city's economy and many fine structures from this era still stand as testament to the wealth of York. The railways of the 1800s played a big part in growth too, with York Station a leading national hub for rail transport and engineering. Among the products that arrived in York were cocoa and sugar; Terry's and Rowntree's were to make York a byword for confectionery production. York truly is England's historic tale in microcosm.

Today, most of the industry has gone and York's economy predominantly relies on financial and legal services and – of course – tourism.

Culture

It is not hard to find culture of all descriptions in York, only difficult to know where to begin. The **Castle Museum** offers an almost literal trip down memory lane in its recreated streets of yore, while **York Art Gallery** spans 600 years of fine British and European Art. The mighty **York Minster** is a treasure trove of ecclesiastical artistry and supreme architectural skill, as are many of the lesser-known and lesser-visited churches in the city (see page 31). The medieval **Merchant Adventurers' Hall** and **Barley Hall** both offer beguiling insights into York's domestic and commercial past, while **Fairfax House** skips forward a few centuries to take visitors on a sumptuous journey through the art and furnishings of York's Georgian wealthy. Beyond the city limits, **Castle Howard** offers a prodigious stately venue for outdoor concerts and events, along with a fine collection of art work. Lovers of classical and world music are well served by the York Early Music Festival (see page 8) and concerts of a similar genre that are held at York University's campus (ⓦ www.yorkconcerts.co.uk).

▶ *The shining interior of the Minster*

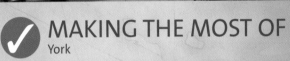

MAKING THE MOST OF
York

Shopping

York has an excellent range of retail outlets, but when this is combined with the fact that many of the stores are housed in medieval stone and half-timbered buildings lining narrow, pedestrianised and cobbled streets, or hidden away down captivating alleyways, its special appeal is obvious. Getting lost while shopping is almost part of the fun, with every corner revealing a new opportunity to browse in exclusive boutiques, find new, vintage or retro clothing, or explore antique shops, bookshops, gift shops and art galleries. To add to the mix, there's a mind-boggling choice of places to rest weary limbs and plastic cards and, being a spiritual home of British confectionery, the streets of York offer a multitude of great places for chocoholics to satisfy their cravings.

Ironically **The Shambles**, now one of the country's most famous and beautifully preserved streets, lacks much in the way of exciting retail therapy. Instead the narrow byways of **Petergate**, **Stonegate** and **Goodramgate** provide a way more satisfying and unique experience. For things a little more eclectic, and predominantly aimed at the younger population, **Fossgate** and **Gillygate** host a good selection of independent shops (including some surprisingly upmarket and well-stocked charity shops to rummage among).

The outdoor **Newgate Market**, located between The Shambles and **Parliament Street**, offers all kinds of budget day-to-day necessities and trinkets amid a lively atmosphere, while national high-street-chain favourites crowd the pedestrian byways of **Coney Street**, Parliament Street and the **Coppergate Centre**.

Just a short journey beyond the city walls, the **York Designer Outlet** offers covered comfort for shoppers among 115 predominantly clothing designer and high-street shops, each offering discounts of up to 60 per cent on normal prices, while **Monks Cross**, just a similar distance to the north, plays host to the generic and larger out-of-town stores.

🔵 *Browsing in the Shambles*

Eating & drinking

Given York is in northern Europe, where climates can be cold, food of the past was customarily served simple, hearty and warming. While happily for some this type of dish is still available, York – like the rest of the UK – has moved on in leaps and bounds to offer a rich range of high-end restaurants and informal bistros, featuring exciting chefs dedicated to creating

🔺 *The stylish interior of Oscar's Wine Bar*

conventional as well as pioneering meals from local produce. Those looking for the delicate doilies and porcelain cake stands of the city's traditional tea shops will also find plenty to keep them enchanted. York's eateries certainly have every culinary base, budget and ambience covered.

For picnics, Newgate Market, Gillygate, Goodramgate or Petergate offer all kinds of local specialities and quality international produce. Take your favourites away and enjoy in the splendid history-packed tranquillity of either Museum Gardens on the lovely riverside, or Dean's Park, tucked away behind the Minster. Or buy food from a choice of eateries on Fossgate and take it to Museum Gardens, where you can join a boat trip (see page 44) and share the idyll with some rather 'pushy' Canadian Geese for company.

Regional specialities to look out for are York Ham, Wensleydale cheese, seafood from Whitby and Yorkshire pudding. Rhubarb, too, is synonymous with Yorkshire; its 'rhubarb triangle' crop (rhubarb that has been 'forced' to give it a distinctive sweet flavour) has been awarded European protected status. For drinkers, Ales of York and the Black Sheep brewery of Masham each produce fine beers from local crops, while another more unlikely local harvest are the grapes grown at nearby Leventhorpe (ⓦ www.englishwineproducers.com), England's most northerly vineyard.

Those heading for the North York Moors and coast will find picnic ingredients in the towns of Whitby, Pickering and Helmsley, which hosts deli foodie favourite Hunters (ⓐ Market Square, Helmsley ⓣ 01439 771307 ⓦ www.huntersofhelmsley.com).

Entertainment

When the sun goes down, York continues to dazzle, and people here certainly know how to enjoy themselves. Pub enthusiasts will find plenty to raise their spirits with one hostelry for every day of the year, many of which are said to be haunted. Micklegate (see page 54) is particularly rich in drinking spots where one can put the world to rights. Those who prefer cool, urbane wine bars and groovy clubs will find a healthy choice, too, particularly along Coney Street, where an assembly of venues boast riverside terraces. For a general overview of upcoming club nights, gigs in the city, and advice on how to buy tickets, visit ⓦ www.yorkgigguide.com. Lovers of indie, folk and rock may have the good fortune to listen to live music among intimate domestic surroundings and an invited audience (ⓦ www.houseconcertsyork.co.uk).

The Biltmore Bar & Grill

EXCESSIVE SPIRITS

York reputedly has more ghosts than any other European city, and every night sees a range of guided walks designed to show visitors the locations of the supernatural and unexplained. There are plenty of fearsome family-friendly tours to choose from, and all generally start at 19.30 and last around 1 hour 15 minutes. No bookings are needed – expect to pay around £4.50 to £5.50 for adults and half that price for children. Two award-winning practitioners are **The Ghost Creeper** (📞 07947 325239 🌐 www.ghostcreeper.com) and **The Ghost Trail** (📞 01904 633276 🌐 www.ghosttrail.co.uk).

The **Grand Opera House** (see page 68) and **Theatre Royal** (see page 56) open their doors to a vibrant and rich programme of touring stage performances, while **City Screen** and **The Basement** (see page 56) offer cinematic art house and more contemporary, challenging stage performances. During the long days of summer, well-known plays are performed outdoors around the city, with the grassy parklands of Museum Gardens a well-used favourite for alfresco dramas. Tickets for these and theatre performances can be sourced from either their respective box offices, from the **York Visitor Centre** (see page 93) or online 🌐 www.visityork.org

Street performers have been entertaining local citizens for centuries. Today, examples of the bizarre, charming, or sometimes just ho-hum, can be enjoyed throughout the year on Parliament Street, St Helen's Square, Stonegate and Petergate.

Sport & relaxation

Cycling & walking

For fresh country air and wide open spaces, the North York Moors can hardly be beaten: they are crisscrossed by 2,300 km (1,437 miles) of country and coastal paths and tracks popular with hikers, walkers and cyclists (ⓦ www.moortoseacycle.net) in need of some off-road adventure.

Fishing

Coastal Whitby provides a choice of fishing opportunities, such as kayak, shore and boat fishing, as well as wreck and reef trips (ⓦ www.whitbyfishingtrips.co.uk or ⓦ www.whitbyseaanglers.co.uk).

Football

For football fans, **York City FC** – even though it is currently languishing at the lower end of the league – does offer a professional soccer fix. ⓐ Kit Kat Crescent ❶ 01904 624447 ⓦ www.ycfc.net ❶ Admission charge

Golf

Pike Hills Golf Club (ⓐ Tadcaster Road, Askham Bryan ⓦ www.pikehillsgolfclub.co.uk) offers a delightful 18-hole parkland and wilderness course; while **Fulford Golf Club**, close to the city centre, allows visiting guests on to its highly regarded course on Mondays and Fridays (ⓐ Heslington Lane ❶ 01904 413579 ⓦ www.fulfordgolfclub.co.uk).

Horse racing

Alongside its impressive history, culture and nightlife, York is also famous for horse racing, with some major meetings taking place between May and October. ⓐ Bishopthorpe Road ⓣ 01904 620911 ⓦ www.yorkracecourse.co.uk ⓝ Bus: From the train station on race days ⓘ Admission charge

Watersports

Fans of watersports will find all kinds of sailing and kayaking opportunities at **Allerthorpe Park** (ⓦ www.allerthorpelakelandpark.co.uk), or can simply cheer participants from the banks during the regattas and themed festivals on the River Ouse (ⓦ www.yorkfestivals.com). It might come as a surprise to some, but surfing off the North Yorkshire coast is very well regarded (ⓦ www.surfshacks.co.uk/yorkshire-surf-guide). For those who prefer to unwind by the river and watch the aquatic world go by, Museum Garden, War Memorial Gardens and Tower Gardens all hit the chill-out spot.

⬥ *Packed stands at York races*

Accommodation

Given York's popularity, it's no surprise that there is a good choice of accommodation to suit every pocket and expectation. However, as one of the world's 'must-see' places, prices can be higher than the national average and rooms difficult to come by in the summer and at weekends, especially during a festival or local race meeting, and in the run-up to Christmas. Arriving without a reservation could therefore be risky: there might be little or nothing in the way of choice and probably eye-wateringly high tariffs to boot. Booking in advance for accommodations in and around the centre of York is always recommended; if possible, staying during the week rather than over weekends could make for substantial cost savings. If this is not possible, head to the York Visitor Centre (see page 93) and they will be happy to help find a bed for the night.

Most of the hotels are clustered within or around the city walls, though Tadcaster Road to the south hosts a good range too as it runs past the racecourse. Small B&Bs and budget hotels tend to be located outside the city walls in the surrounding suburbs, though many are just a 15- or 20-minute walk into the heart of the city.

HOTELS

Holiday Inn Express £ Just under 5 km (3 miles) from the city centre, this budget business and tourist hotel in York's northern suburbs is consistent with the rest of the chain in its modern décor, comforts and facilities. ⓐ Malton Road ☏ 01904 438660 ⓦ www.hiexpress.com

The Churchill Hotel ££ Historic hotel housed in a Georgian period mansion filled with a blend of period, contemporary and quirky furnishings. Despite its grandness, this is a friendly place just a five-minute walk from the Minster and has a guest car park in its grounds. ⓐ 65 Bootham ⓣ 01904 644456 ⓦ www.churchillhotel.com

Dean Court Hotel ££ Probably the best location in York, the historic façades reveal modern designer accommodation within the shadow of the spectacular Minster. Very friendly staff, an award-winning restaurant (see page 54) and a host of features in the rooms (including international electrical plug sockets) make for a truly rewarding stay. ⓐ Duncombe Place ⓣ 01904 625082 ⓦ www.deancourt-york.co.uk

Marriott Hotel ££ Close to the racecourse and just a 20-minute walk to the city centre; tranquil landscaped gardens and old-world charm meets 21st-century, 4-star business and pleasure facilities that include a spa and pool. ⓐ Tadcaster Road ⓣ 01904 701000 ⓦ www.marriott.co.uk

The Cedar Court Grand Hotel & Spa £££ Just beyond the city walls, this recently converted railway headquarters is now a luxurious hotel that offers a personal butler service for its guests. A roof garden for relaxation and vaulted spa for pampering complete the lavish experience. ⓐ Station Rise ⓣ 0845 409 6430 ⓦ www.cedarcourtgrand.co.uk

GUEST HOUSES

Aaron Guest House £ Warm and tastefully decorated family-run accommodation, set in a quiet location yet just a short walk to the city's attractions. Free parking and 24-hour access make this an excellent choice in its price bracket. ⓐ 42 Bootham Crescent ⓣ 07980 556898 ⓦ www.aaronyork.co.uk

City Guest House £ Small guesthouse offering six well-equipped en-suite rooms (including one on the ground floor), free parking and just a short walk from York's central attractions. ⓐ 68 Monkgate ⓣ 01904 622483 ⓦ www.cityguesthouse.co.uk

Ashbourne House ££ Just a short distance to both the city centre and university campus, the six modern, well-equipped, bright and airy rooms make this a popular choice for college visitors and tourists. ⓐ 139 Fulford Road ⓣ 01904 639912 ⓦ www.ashbournehouseyork.co.uk

HOSTELS

Ace Hotel £ An impressive Georgian façade conceals a wonderful array of original features in its bedrooms and dorms, and provides a number of facilities and perks – such as a sauna – not normally associated with hostels. Close to both the station and attractions. ⓐ 88–90 Micklegate ⓣ 01904 627720 ⓦ www.acehotelyork.co.uk

The Bar Convent ££ Opt to stay in the oldest, still occupied convent in England for a totally unique experience. Faith is not an issue in this beautiful Georgian listed building offering comfortable B&B (some rooms en-suite), plenty of facilities, all just a short stroll from the centre. A dedicated museum, shop and café also form part of the experience. ⓐ 17 Blossom Street ⓣ 01904 643238 ⓦ www.bar-convent.org.uk

CAMPING & CARAVANNING

York Caravan Park £ Located within the city's outer ring road, this well-equipped and large-pitch site comes with a fishing lake, nature reserve, nearby country pub and is well suited for journeys to the city, the North York Moors and Whitby.
ⓐ Stockton Lane ⓣ 01904 424222
ⓦ www.yorkcaravanstorage.com Ⓝ Bus: 840

York Yurts £ Take a short, 15-minute journey east of the city to discover spacious and sumptuous Mongolian canvas comfort alongside a communal marquee, all surrounded by rich pasture and woodland scenery. ⓐ Tadpole Cottage, Barmby Moor
ⓣ 01759 380901 ⓦ www.yorkyurts.com Ⓝ Bus: 746, X46

THE BEST OF YORK

Such is the variety of York and its densely-packed historical attractions that anyone with even the remotest interest in the past will be enthralled by the city. A range of sights vies for attention and it is well worth the effort to draw up a plan of attack before arriving.

TOP 10 ATTRACTIONS

- **Medieval streets** Enjoy ambling and exploring some of best-preserved and most evocative streets and alleys in the world (see page 43).

- **York Castle Museum** This museum seems to cover almost every aspect of life and includes recreated streets with 'live' shops. Located in a former court and prison (see page 59).

- **The Minster** Not just one of the grandest cathedrals in Europe, but one of the finest buildings, with excellent basement archaeology and roof views (see page 45).

- **Jorvik Viking Centre** Part Disney-ride, part excellent museum and a real winner with families interested in York's Viking past (see page 57).

- **North York Moors** Captured in film, TV and literature, the moors offer breathtaking wild scenery and exquisitely picturesque villages (see page 80).

- **National Railway Museum** A massive collection spanning 200 years of railway history – and all for free (see page 43).

- **Christmas** A magical time in the city, the atmosphere is redolent of Dickens with guaranteed 'snow', street markets, ice events and all kinds of festive fun (see page 9).

- **Castle Howard** The magnificent palatial home of the Howard family, along with its vast gardens, provides a fascinating day out (see page 71).

- **Visit to Whitby** This traditional harbour town, seaside resort and fishing port spans the River Esk and is a winner with all ages (see page 85).

- **Walking the walls** Free and fascinating, the ramparts of the medieval city walls offer a great overview of York (see page 30).

◗ *Boats on the Ouse in springtime*

Suggested itineraries

HALF-DAY: YORK IN A HURRY

When time is of the essence, head first to the Minster and marvel at the immense medieval engineering and craftsmanship that went into this mammoth dedication (see page 45). Next, take to the nearby city walls for the 90-minute circuitous walk above the bustling city to get marvellous vistas and a historic overview (see page 30).

1 DAY: TIME TO SEE A LITTLE MORE

A complete day allows time for the above, including visits to the Minster's crypt and roof. Make a visit to one of the numerous museums in York, such as the Castle Museum (see page 59), which has a good all-round range of exhibits for all ages. In between, enjoy lunch at one of the two Bettys tea rooms (see page 52) for a taste of old-world charm and indulgence (given their popularity, it is worth getting there early).

2–3 DAYS: SHORT CITY-BREAK

Start by taking to the city walls and mulling over the various information boards and museums along the way, or join one of the guided open-top bus tours or river cruises. The Railway Museum (see page 43), Fairfax House (see page 60), Merchant Adventurers' Hall (see page 60) and Jorvik Viking Centre (see page 57) are all definitely worthy of some lingering attention, and the luxury of having a few days means that there will be time to relax in the parks with a picnic, or perhaps even to hire a small motorboat and take to the river (see page 59). Exploring the numerous medieval streets and alleys and discovering hidden gems is a pleasure in itself (see page 43), as is heading to the bars lining the riverside for an early evening cocktail before joining one of the spookily intriguing ghost walks (see page 19).

LONGER: ENJOYING YORK TO THE FULL

As well as enjoying the firm favourites above, more time in the city means a chance to uncover some of York's lesser-known attractions, such as **Barley Hall** (see page 45), **Quilt Museum and Gallery** (see page 46), **York City Art Gallery** (see page 49), **DIG** (see page 46) and the **Cold War Bunker** (see page 69). Beyond the city, make the two-hour journey to the seaside at Whitby (see page 85), stopping on the way to soak in the wild rural tranquillity of the North York Moors (see page 80).

△ York City Art Gallery

Something for nothing

With so many things to see and do, visiting York can be an expensive business; however, there still remains a good choice of free things to enjoy. The most obvious are the Norman city walls, which provide over 3 km (1¾ miles) of sightseeing high above the teeming city. Back on ground level, just turn up outside the City Art Gallery at the appointed time to enjoy a free, two-hour guided **walking tour** of the city. (🕐 10.15, 14.15 daily, Apr–Oct; 10.15, Nov–Mar). Alternatively simply stroll at your own pace through the warren of preserved historic streets such as The Shambles, Petergate and Stonegate, also uncovering the city's hidden profusion of intriguing alleys and yards known locally as 'Snickleways'. To the south of the city is the lovely 1.6-km (1-mile) riverside walk starting at Tower Gardens.

Beyond the city, North Yorkshire offers priceless stretches of beautiful open countryside and coastal scenery that mixes fine beaches and dramatic cliff faces.

THE SHAMBLES
The name Shambles derives from the medieval *Shamel* (booth or bench) or *Flesshammel*, meaning butcher's bench, since in the past it was home to butchers' shops and houses. Many of these exterior counters, along with hanging meat hooks, are still visible in this street, which dates back at least 900 years and is the best preserved of its kind in Europe.

When it rains

This being northern England, unfortunately rain can be part of everyday life, but in York there are a plethora of places in which to take shelter and keep oneself amused. Apart from the big-hitting attractions, York also has a fine legacy of often unnoticed medieval churches, each offering a place of undiscovered and fascinating peace. **St Denys** (ⓐ Walmgate), **Holy Trinity** (ⓐ Goodramgate) and **St Michael-le-Belfry** (ⓐ Petergate), where local boy and future gunpowder-plotter Guy Fawkes was baptised, are just a small selection. The small **Shrine of Margaret Clitherow** (ⓐ The Shambles) is a sacred and fascinating destination that tells the story of one woman's fight against religious intolerance in the 16th century. For something a little more up to date, the church of **York St Mary's** offers space for a rolling programme of contemporary art installations. ⓐ Castlegate ⓦ www.yorkstmarys.org.uk

For those interested in the elixir of beer, **York Brewery** (ⓐ 12 Toft Green ⓣ 01904 621162 ⓦ www.york-brewery.co.uk ⓘ Admission charge) offers daily tours with all participants rewarded with generous samples at its conclusion.

On arrival

ARRIVING
By air
York has no airport to call its own, but there are a number of smaller regional airports not far from the city: Leeds/Bradford, Robin Hood Airport Doncaster Sheffield and Durham Tees Valley Airport all offer domestic and international services. Alternatively, Manchester Airport supplies a good selection of full service routes further afield (see page 90).

By rail
The city is very well served by rail, with its station just a 10-minute walk from the city centre. Routes serve all major hubs in the UK, with both London and Edinburgh particularly well connected (see page 90).

By road
Arriving in York by road can be a little more troublesome. Inner and outer ring roads exist but are only dual carriageways to the south and east, meaning the approaches from north and west can get particularly clogged. Once on the ring roads, getting to the city centre itself can take a while, despite the short distances. Parking in the centre too can be challenging (particularly between 11.00 and 16.00) and expensive, so an alternative is to make use of the Park and Ride schemes scattered around the outskirts (see map page 70).

FINDING YOUR FEET

Given that York's centre is almost completely enclosed by its historic wall, there is a little chance of wandering off the beaten path and into any kind of trouble. Within the walls the narrow streets can sometimes be packed with people, though most of the attractions, shops, bars and restaurants are situated in a pedestrianised area to the east of the river, so traffic is not an issue in these parts. As in other major tourist destinations, the vast visitor numbers do attract criminals and petty 'chancers', and these people will pick the pockets of the unprepared and distracted. Just act sensibly, and follow your instincts if you feel uncomfortable about people or places. Beyond the city walls there are some less than salubrious areas that offer little reward for the visitor, and these are generally best left off the itinerary – by day and by night. The North Yorkshire Police (see page 91) has responsibility for tackling crime and disorder at a local level, and the city has no more issues with crime and safety than any of its European counterparts.

ORIENTATION

Though the network of celebrated streets, particularly in the north of the city centre, can mean it is possible to find yourself temporarily mislaid, the compact nature of York means it is never a serious issue. In fact, wandering off track in these highways and byways can be part of the joyous adventure of discovery. The Minster has been a gigantic beacon for the lost (figuratively and literally) for centuries; it towers over York's heart and is still visible from just about every corner of the city,

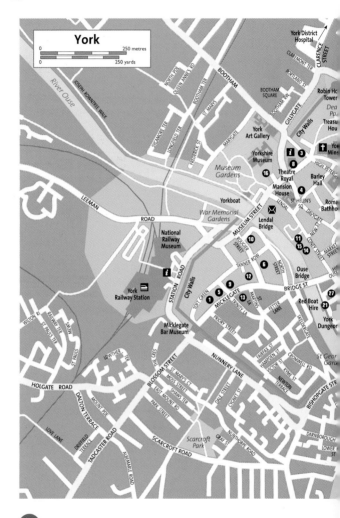

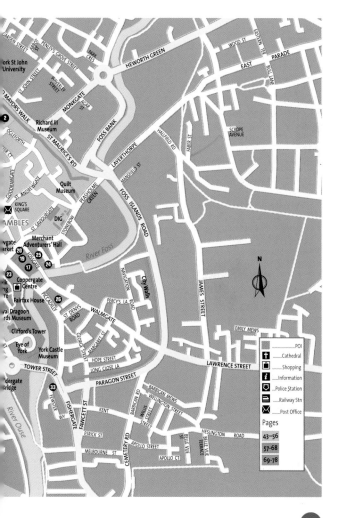

while the encircling walls and River Ouse, which cuts through the centre, ensure that straying too far off course is unlikely. It should take no more than 15 minutes to walk from north to south or east to west at a gentle pace.

GETTING AROUND

Without a doubt, getting around the centre of York is best done on foot. There is no metro or tram system in the city so it's left to buses to skirt passengers around the edges of the predominantly pedestrianised centre and away into the suburbs and towns such as Helmsley, Pickering and Whitby and into the countryside of the North York Moors.

There is no one dedicated bus station in York, rather a series of major bus stops handling the bulk of the services, with the largest to be found outside the railway station. Working from

WHAT'S IN A NAME?

For first-time visitors and those unused to medieval street names, York's thoroughfares can seem a little confusing – and intriguing. The word 'gate' as found in 40 street names throughout the city – Coppergate and Swinegate among them – derives from the Viking word for street, gata. The term 'bar' is found in the names given to the four gateways placed around the surrounding city walls, Bootham Bar, Monk Bar, Walmgate Bar and Micklegate Bar. These were the sites of the former bars, or barriers, that were used to control access to the city.

north to south, other major bus hubs are located at St Leonard's Place, Rougier Street, Micklegate, Low Ousegate, Piccadilly and Blossom Street, where information on routes and times are all available. Many of the buses are wheelchair accessible and protocol for joining a bus is the same here as in the rest of the UK. Simply raise an arm to signal to the driver that you want to be picked up, and on boarding state your destination and what sort of ticket you need (single, return, day pass, etc.). You will have to pay cash, and the correct change is generally appreciated. Note that there are a number of different bus

⬥ *York's train station*

companies operating in the city and tickets are not transferable between them. For a range of unlimited day and seasonal bus travel passes for individuals and families ask the bus driver, contact **Traveline Yorkshire** (ⓣ 0871 200 2233 ⓦ www.yorkshiretravel.net) or visit the York Visitor Centre (see page 93).

Plus Bus offers cheap day passes for all bus services and can be bought at the railway station, but it is limited to the city and suburbs. ⓦ www.plusbus.info

Taxis

There is no shortage of licensed cabs in York, which can either be hailed on the street or collected at ranks that can be found at (from north to south) St Leonard's Place, St Saviourgate, the railway station, Rougier Street, Piccadilly and Tower Street. ⓣ 01904 623332.

There are plentiful fleets of minicabs too, but – as in the rest of the UK – these must be booked in advance; it is against the law for them to collect passengers off the streets.
Fleetways Taxis ⓣ 01904 654333 ⓦ www.fleetways.co.uk
Telecars Taxis ⓣ 01904 424646 ⓦ www.telecarstaxis.co.uk
Stream Line Taxis ⓣ 01904 638833
ⓦ www.streamlinetaxisyork.co.uk

Cycling

York is one of the elite few places that have been awarded Cycling City Status, and getting around the extensive network of off-road tracks and on-road lanes – along with plenty of secure parking – makes for safe access in and around the centre. Free route maps are available from York's Visitor Information Centre (see page 93).

Autohorn supplies bicycles for all ages, accompanied by all the equipment required; these can be hired for approximately £10 per 24 hours. ⓐ Europcar Hire Office, York Railway Station ⓦ www.autohorn.co.uk ⓔ enquiries@autohorn.co.uk ⓛ 08.00–20.30 Mon–Sat, 09.00–20.30 Sun

🔺 Explore on foot and get close to the city's many street performers

Car hire

Hiring a car to navigate the compact city centre is an unnecessary expense and it can be a nuisance when it comes to parking; but if public transport isn't practical, renting a car might be useful for getting beyond the central city area and out into the surrounding suburbs and countryside. Costs and terms do vary, but a rough figure for one day's rental on a four-door intermediate class vehicle should be between £45 and £55.

Avis ⓐ 3–7 Layerthorpe ❶ 0844 581 0014 ⓦ www.avis.co.uk

Enterprise ⓐ 15 Foss Island Road ❶ 01904 623000
ⓦ www.enterprise.co.uk

Europcar ⓐ York Railway Station ❶ 01904 656161
ⓦ www.europcar.co.uk

Minster Self Drive ⓐ 111 Micklegate ❶ 01904 644333
ⓦ www.minsterselfdrive.co.uk

JOIN THE CLUB

One alternative to standard car hire is to join a pay-as-you-go car club scheme. York Council has endorsed such a project and once membership formalities have been completed and an annual fee of £50 paid, eco-friendly vehicles can be rented by the hour, day or longer from a choice of locations in the city centre, university and selected suburbs. ❶ 0113 350 3930 ⓦ www.citycarclub.co.uk
ⓔ york@citycarclub.co.uk

▶ *Constantine the Great: Roman Emperor in York*

CONSTANTINE BY THIS SIGN CONQUER

THE CITY OF
York

Introduction

Centuries of town planning and historic defensive needs have made navigation around the city of York easy today. For the purposes of this guidebook, the city has been divided into three easily distinguished areas to make it easy for the visitor to find their way around. The city centre area has been divided on a roughly horizontal access into two sections. These northern and southern areas are separated by one street that, while changing name along its route – starting in the southwest as Micklegate, it is variously named Bridge Street, Low Ousegate, Coppergate, Pavement, The Stonebow and Peasholme Green in the northeast – remains quite distinctive. In City centre north are the vast bulk of narrow medieval streets, hotels, bars, restaurants and shopping. In City centre south, the city takes on a newer, more open feel, playing host to most of the riverside activities and a selection of famous attractions.

The third section (Outside the city centre) looks at attractions outside the immediate centre and up to around 50 km (30 miles) away, including the racecourse, a selection of out-of-town museums and attractions, and wonderful villages. Many of these sights require a car or bus transportation to reach (see page 37).

City centre north

This area forms the focal point of York's Roman and medieval heart and is characterised by its warren of higgledy-piggledy streets and unique shops. The Minster dominates. This is also home to the main Post Office (ⓐ 22 Lendal), the Visitor Information Centre (see page 93) and the banks. Some of the sights lie just beyond the northern and western extent of the city walls.

SIGHTS & ATTRACTIONS

National Railway Museum

The 'big daddy' of all rail museums in the country, this enormous cathedral to the world of trains features railway icons and thousands of artefacts covering its social, engineering and design aspects. There are footplates to stand on, carriages to walk through and royal trains to peer in at. For children there are a series of trails to follow, as well as activities and demonstrations through the school holidays. ⓐ Leeman Road ⓣ 0844 815 3139 ⓦ www.nrm.org.uk ⓛ 10.00–18.00 daily ⓝ A dedicated **road train** to the museum leaves Duncombe Place every 30 minutes (ⓛ 11.15–16.15 daily (summer only); 11.15–16.15 Sat & Sun (Jan–Mar))

Roman Bathhouse

In the cellars of a rather ordinary pub, the steam baths used by Roman soldiers and citizens have been opened to the public. A walkway has been created to view its remains alongside a

collection of everyday Roman objects. ❷ 9 St Sampson's Square
❶ 01904 620455 ❶ Admission charge

Yorkboat

Relaxing and informative 45-minute river cruises along the Ouse
with commentary from the captain on York's riverside past.
Boats come with open and with enclosed, heated decks, toilets
and bar. Floodlit evening and dinner cruises also take place
during the summer months. ❷ Lendal Bridge ❶ 01904 628324
Ⓦ www.yorkboat.co.uk ❶ Daily Feb–Nov ❶ Admission charge

● *Back to the steam age at the National Railway Museum*

York Minster

Perhaps the jewel in York's crown, this monumental Gothic edifice is a space of such extraordinary beauty that it is difficult to comprehend it was created over five centuries ago. The stained glass is breathtaking in its rarity and finery, particularly the great east window. There are free guided tours once inside (🕐 09.00–15.00 Mon–Sat), as well as behind-the-scenes stained-glass conservation tours (🕐 14.00 Wed & Fri 🛈 Tour charge). In the Undercroft (beneath the floor of the Minster) are remains of former Roman occupation together with foundations from much earlier church constructions (🛈 Separate admission charge). For the fit there is a 275 narrow-step climb to the top of the central tower for breathtaking views across the medieval streets and countryside beyond (🛈 Separate admission charge). ⓐ Deansgate 🕿 0844 939 0016 🌐 www.yorkminster.org 🕐 09.00–17.30 Mon–Sat, 12.00–15.45 Sun 🛈 Admission charge; closed to sightseers Good Friday, Easter Sunday and certain days when only open for services.

CULTURE

Barley Hall

Once home to the medieval mayors of York and the Priors of Nostell, this lovingly restored building has been designed to tell the tale of York during the hall's occupation and is particularly fun and rewarding for children. ⓐ 2 Coffee Yard, off Stonegate 🕿 01904 615505 🌐 www.barleyhall.org.uk 🕐 10.00–16.00 daily (summer); 10.00–15.00 daily (winter) 🛈 Admission charge

DIG

Entertaining and educational local archaeological centre, predominantly aimed at children, with lots to see and the chance to get their hands dirty. Adults will find the site tours a fascinating insight into 2,000 years of history and be able to enjoy the continued archaeological excavations taking place. ⓐ St Saviour's Church, St Saviourgate ☏ 01904 615505 ⓦ www.digyork.co.uk 🕐 10.00–16.00 daily ❶ Admission charge. Tours must be booked in advance

Mansion House

Striking official residence of the Lord Mayor of York, where for the past 300 years civic guests have been entertained in its grand and lavish interiors. Tours are available on Fridays and Saturdays. ⓐ St Helens Square ☏ 01904 552036

Quilt Museum and Gallery

A unique museum and gallery dedicated to the art of quilt-making and textiles, featuring a rolling programme of visiting exhibitions of the craft. ⓐ Peasholme Green ☏ 01904 613242 ⓦ www.quiltmuseum.org.uk 🕐 10.00–16.00 Tues–Sat (Oct–Mar), closed Sat & Sun; 10.00–16.00 Mon–Sat (Apr–Sept), closed Sun ❶ Admission charge

Richard III Museum

Tiny and quirky museum that focuses on the much-debated 15th-century monarch Richard III, where he is put on trial and visitors are left to decide whether he was guilty of crimes such as the murder of the 'princes in the Tower', or whether history

◔ *The Minster's impressive Gothic façade*

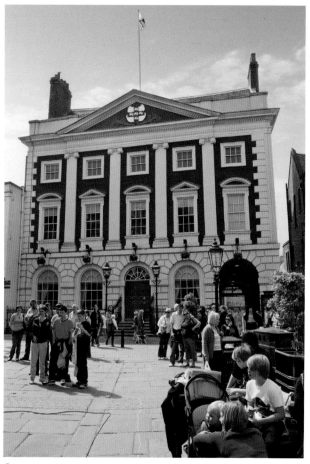

⬥ *Mansion House: the Mayor's official residence*

has just given him a bad press. Housed in York's largest medieval gatehouse, still retaining many of its original features as a former prison and police house. ⓐ Monk Bar ⓣ 01904 634191 ⓦ www.richardiiimuseum.co.uk ⓛ 09.30–16.00 daily (Nov–Feb); 09.00–17.00 daily (Mar–Oct) ⓝ Bus: 12, 13, 181 ⓘ Admission charge and no disabled access

Treasurer's House

From the remains of a Roman road in the cellar, to the Edwardian servants' quarters in the eaves, this is not only one of York's most beautiful homes, but also one of its most historically diverse. Home to a private collection of art and furnishings, and to a number of ghostly tales, a lovely garden adds to the allure. ⓐ Minster Yard ⓣ 01904 624247 ⓦ www.nationaltrust.org.uk ⓛ 11.00–16.30 Sun–Thur (Apr–Oct); 11.00–15.00 Sun–Thur (Nov) ⓘ Admission charge

York Art Gallery

This gallery houses a relatively small collection of paintings and ceramics over two floors spanning six centuries of local, national and international work from Dutch and Italian masters. ⓐ Exhibition Square ⓣ 01904 687687 ⓦ www.yorkartgallery.org.uk ⓛ 10.00–17.00 daily

Yorkshire Museum

Following major refurbishment, five new galleries showcase some of the best archaeological treasures in the country, including prime Anglo-Saxon and Viking finds. Astronomy and its history are also comprehensively covered and include an original 19th-century observatory. Elsewhere visitors will find interesting displays of rare geology, animals and birds.

🅐 Museum Gardens ☎ 01904 687687
🅦 www.yorkshiremuseum.org.uk 🕒 10.00–17.00 daily (Observatory 🕒 11.30–14.30 Sat only) ❗ Admission charge (free entry for a year after purchase)

RETAIL THERAPY

Shopaholics will find this area of York the most satisfying. The daily Newgate Market is situated here, offering all kinds of produce, jewellery, clothing and day-to-day necessities. Close by, Parliament Street and parallel Coney Street hosts big-name stores including York's very own **Browns** department store (🅐 Davygate 🅦 www.brownsofyork.co.uk). But the real jewels in the city's shopping crown are the unique gift, clothing and accessory shops to be found in the historic streets to the south and west of the Minster, with Stonegate and Petergate especially rewarding destinations.

TAKING A BREAK

The Blake Head Café £ ❶ Vegetarian and vegan café housed at the back of one of the city's well-known bookshops. Regularly winning awards, the food – though simple – is consistently well prepared and can be accompanied by a range of organic wines and herbal teas. 🅐 104 Micklegate ☎ 01904 623767
🅦 www.theblakehead.co.uk 🕒 09.00–17.00 Mon–Sat, 10.00–17.00 Sun

Grays Court £ ❷ An English country home in the heart of the city offering hot drinks and light snacks in the splendour and refinement of its Long Gallery or the tranquillity of its walled garden. ❸ Chapter House Street ❶ 01904 612613 Ⓦ www.grayscourtyork.com Ⓛ 10.00–18.00 daily

The House of Avalon £ ❸ Little tea shop with a big difference. Housed in the back room of a vintage clothing and accessory store, tasty desserts are served to the accompaniment of classic movies shown on the wall. ❸ 5 High Petergate ❶ 01904 622055

⬥ *Bustling Stonegate*

Ⓦ www.thehouseofavalon.org.uk Ⓛ 10.00–17.00 Tues–Sun
(closed Mon, except for bank holidays)

Little Bettys £ ❹ People travel from far and wide to queue to
enjoy this extraordinary phenomena. There are two café
branches in the city, with this being the little sister to the
flagship café around the corner. Downstairs is a shop selling
cakes, teas and gifts, while the upstairs café is a celebration of
bone china, cream teas and cucumber sandwiches, all served in
an evocative 'Edwardian' ambience. Ⓐ 46 Stonegate
Ⓣ 01904 622865 Ⓦ www.bettys.co.uk Ⓛ 10.00–17.30 Sun–Fri,
09.00–17.50 Sat

Yorkshire Food Company £ ❺ Large deli, café and cookery
shop serving the best in local sweet and savoury produce,
including a fine selection of wine and beer in its cellar.
Ⓐ 130–134 Micklegate Ⓣ 01904 630497
Ⓦ www.theyorkshirefoodcompany.com Ⓛ 08.30–16.30 Mon–Sat,
11.00–16.30 Sun

AFTER DARK

RESTAURANTS
Kapadokya 50 £ ❻ Featuring regional authentic Turkish cuisine
cooked on its open grill. The warm and charismatic staff and
quality of the food make for an enjoyable and relaxed
experience. Ⓐ 24 George Hudson Street Ⓣ 01904 622500
Ⓦ www.kapadokya-restaurant.co.uk Ⓛ 12.00–14.30 & 17.00–
23.30 Mon–Sat, 12.00–22.30 Sun

La Vecchia Scuola £ ❼ Stand-out Italian restaurant housed in a former girls' school and offering delightful views from its pastel interiors and conservatory across to the Minster. A laid-back, affable ambience accompanies pasta and pizza favourites alongside chef specialities. ⓐ 62 Low Petergate ❶ 01904 644600 ⓦ www.la-vecchia-scuola.co.uk ❷ 09.30–23.30 daily

⬥ *Queuing for tea and cakes at Bettys*

D.C.H. **££** **❽** British and Mediterranean cuisine created from local produce take centre stage in this well-regarded and award-winning haven of fine dining. All this is complemented by friendly service and some glorious views of the illuminated Minster from several of its tables during the evening.
ⓐ Duncombe Place ❶ 01904 625082
ⓦ www.deancourt-york.co.uk ❺ 12.00–14.00 & 19.00–21.30 daily

PUBS & BARS

Brigantes **❾** Amongst a plethora of places to drink along Micklegate, this highly regarded, laid-bare pub takes its great choice of beers very seriously. ⓐ 114 Micklegate ❶ 01904 675355
ⓦ www.markettowntaverns.co.uk

MICKLEGATE RUN

This medieval cobbled street runs downhill from the western entrance to the city to the river and hosts approximately 16 bars and pubs to make up one of the country's most famous pub crawls. The start is generally considered to be on Blossom Street (the extension of Micklegate, just outside the city walls), from which point students, galloping stag nights and racy hen parties visit each and every watering hole on their way back to the city centre. This long-established endurance event fortunately offers a selection of restaurants and takeaways en route at which to take on solid fuel and water.

The Maltings  Describing itself as a pub 'for grownups', this traditional inn offers an array of international and local beers and ciders, as well as a fine whisky menu, all served up in exceedingly homely and convivial surroundings. Live music is featured on Monday and Tuesday nights. ⓐ Tanners Moat ⓣ 01904 655387 ⓦ www.maltings.co.uk ⓛ 11.00–23.00 Mon–Sat, noon–22.30 Sun

Revolution ⓫ From a choice of waterfront terrace bars, this one stands out for its quirky décor within an imposing former local newspaper building. Vodka and partying a particular speciality, this trendy modern haunt is gentle during the day for a break, and lively with dance cuts come dusk. ⓐ Coney Street ⓣ 01904 676054 ⓦ www.revolution-bars.co.uk/york

CLUBS & VENUES

The Parish ⓬ Converted church that is now one of the most popular night spots in York, particularly at weekends. It employs much of the ecclesiastical architecture and fittings to good effect, including a gallery from which to watch the sin unfolding on the dance floor below. Food served through the day. ⓐ 2 Micklegate ⓣ 01904 643424

Hub Nightclub ⓭ This enduring 'down and dirty' basement nightclub, formerly Ziggys, entertains the young throughout the week in a series of theme nights covering indie, rock and dance, and special performances by guest DJs. Special discounts for students. ⓐ 53–55 Micklegate ⓣ 01904 620602 ⓦ www.ziggysnightclub.com

CINEMA & THEATRE

The Basement ⓮ Set beneath City Screen (see below), this intimate venue plays host to a wide collection of live performances, including comedy, music, performance and open mike. ⓐ 13–17 Coney Street ⓣ 01904 612940 ⓦ www.thebasementyork.co.uk

City Screen ⓯ Centrally located cinema showing the best in box-office smashes, international and art-house screenings complemented by terraced licensed café/bar with picturesque views over the river. ⓐ 13–17 Coney Street ⓣ 0871 704 2054 ⓦ www.picturehouses.co.uk

York Theatre Royal ⓰ A Grade II listed theatre just outside the city walls, presenting a full programme of touring productions including ballet, comedy, drama and concerts. ⓐ St Leonard's Place ⓣ 01904 623568 ⓦ www.yorktheatreroyal.co.uk

City centre south

Less retail, more sights and attractions, the narrow and crowded medieval streets to the north of the centre give way to slightly larger byways, more open public spaces and some of the city's most popular attractions, including the Jorvik Viking Centre and the chilling York Dungeon. While this area may not offer the same in the way of chic bars and clubs as its northern neighbour, it does have some interesting pubs as well as some excellent eateries.

SIGHTS & ATTRACTIONS

Clifford's Tower

Though there is no longer a great deal to be seen inside, this was a former castle of William the Conqueror, a Royal Mint and prison. The famous city landmark was also the location for a dark episode: the mass murder of York's Jewish population during the 12th century. ➋ Tower Street ⓦ www.english-heritage.org.uk ⓛ 10.00–18.00 daily (summer); 10.00–16.00 daily (winter) ⓘ Admission charge. Access is quite limited and involves 55 steps and uneven and precarious paths

Jorvik Viking Centre

This great centre combines a little Disney-inspired magic with a good splash of interactive museum. A full sensory subterranean ride (including the smells and sounds of Viking life) first takes you through York's Viking streets before passing genuine archaeological troves, displaying some of the 40,000 objects discovered in the dig on this site in 1979–81. In the museum, lots of enthusiastic staff are on hand to demonstrate a variety of Viking crafts and skills. Popular with school parties, queuing should sometimes be expected, though there are often costumed characters outside creating an entertaining distraction. ⓐ Coppergate ❶ 01904 615505 ⓦ www.jorvik-viking-centre.co.uk ❶ 10.00–17.00 daily (summer); 10.00–16.00 (winter), closed over Christmas period ❶ Admission charge

⬥ *York Dungeon: not for the faint-hearted*

Red boat hire

Simple to operate and ideal for a picnic, this is an opportunity to take to the wheel of an eight-person motorboat for an hour and explore York's historic watery highway. ⓐ King's Staith Landing ⓣ 01904 628324 ⓦ www.yorkboat.co.uk ⓛ Daily Feb–Nov ⓘ Admission charge

York Castle Museum

Best known for its enclosed recreated Victorian streets and the host of informed characters inhabiting them, the museum also displays one of the largest and most joyous collections of everyday ephemera in Britain. This is also home to the recently redesigned Castle Prison Museum, based in the original prison house and cells, where Dick Turpin spent his remaining days before being executed nearby. Plenty for children as well as adults to see and do. ⓐ Eye of York ⓣ 01904 687687 ⓦ www.yorkcastlemuseum.org.uk ⓛ 09.30–17.30 daily ⓘ Admission charge (free return entry for 12 months with ticket)

York Dungeon

Plenty of thrills, chills, gore and heart-stopping frights. A world away from rubber bats on elastic, this fright-fest employs enthusiastic actors and technology to recreate despicable tales with absolutely ghoulish relish. Certainly not for younger children or the faint-hearted. ⓐ 12 Clifford Street ⓣ 01904 632599 ⓦ www.thedungeons.com ⓛ 10.30–17.00 (Apr–Sept), 11.00–16.00 (Oct–Mar) ⓘ Admission charge. Children under 16 must be accompanied by an adult

CULTURE

Fairfax House

In the 18th century, York was regarded by London's moneyed élite as an elegant and attractive alternative to the capital. Still one of the finest, most richly decorated Georgian townhouses in Britain, Fairfax House is preserved in all its glory and provides a home for the extraordinary collection of period furniture and clocks that Noel Terry (of Terry's confectionery fame) amassed in his lifetime. ⓐ Castlegate ❶ 01904 655543 ⓦ www.fairfaxhouse.co.uk ⏰ 11.00–14.30 Mon–Thur & Sat, 11.00 & 14.00 Fri (guided tours only), 13.30–16.30 Sun ❶ Admission charge

Merchant Adventurers' Hall

The finest example in England of a guildhall, where traders of the same guild still come together today to meet and do business. Built during the 14th century, this remarkably preserved building hosts fine collections including silver, furniture and art. ⓐ Fossgate ❶ 01904 654818 ⓦ www.theyorkcompany.co.uk ⏰ 09.00–17.00 Mon–Thur, 09.00–15.30 Fri & Sat, 12.00–16.00 Sun (summer); 09.00–15.30 Mon–Sat (winter) ❶ Admission charge. May be closed for special events

Micklegate Bar Museum

Set in the original and main entrance into the city, this is three informative floors covering 800 years of history, recounting with particular relish the macabre past of the gates, where heads of executed prisoners were once displayed. As far as you're likely to get from high-tech presentations, this only adds to the charm and it is a great value experience. ⓐ Micklegate ① 01904 634436 ⓛ 10.00–15.00 daily ① Admission charge

🔺 Explore York's past at the Jorvik Viking Centre

◆ *The 55 steps leading up to Clifford's Tower*

Royal Dragoon Guards Museum

Well-presented and spacious museum revealing over 300 years of the dragoon's history and heritage, and that of the Prince of Wales's Own Regiment of Yorkshire. On show are weaponry, uniforms, standards and a whole of host of related documents and artworks, all complemented by a multimedia presentation. ⓐ 3a Tower Street ⓣ 01904 642036 ⓦ www.rdgmuseum.org.uk ⓛ 09.30–16.30 Mon–Sat ⓘ Admission charge

RETAIL THERAPY

There are fewer shops on this side of the city, though the **Coppergate Centre** (ⓦ www.coppergateshoppingcentre.co.uk) does provide a small collection of partially sheltered high-street shops alongside upmarket department store Fenwick (ⓦ www.fenwick.co.uk). Alternatively Fossgate, leading to Walmgate, is a haven for some of the city's more esoteric, independent stores, such as **Vamps** (ⓣ 01904 675443) for goth/punk clothing and **Purple Haze** (ⓣ 01904 630407) for classic vintage and retro attire.

TAKING A BREAK

The Hairy Fig £ ⓱ Café and deli offering 'fine fodder' to eat in or take away, including choice produce from the region and across the world, and balsamics on tap (buy a bottle or bring your own) all served with enthusiasm and knowledge. ⓐ 38/39 Fossgate ⓣ 01904 654904 ⓦ www.thehairyfig.co.uk

La Place Verte £ ⑱ Excellent Belgian speciality coffee shop with a terrace by the river. It serves light snacks, desserts and delicious hot chocolate that you create yourself from a choice of ingredients served at the table. ⓐ The Motor House, Skeldergate Bridge ❶ 01904 677005 ⓦ www.laplaceverte.co.uk ❶ 11.00–18.00 daily (summer); 10.00–17.00 (winter)

PUBS & BARS

The Bluebell Inn ⑲ Somewhat off the tourist trail, this tiny traditional pub tends to attract the locals who come to enjoy its wonderfully preserved 1900s interior, its fine real ale and simple and hearty food. Football fans might be intrigued to know that this is where York City FC were officially formed in 1922. ⓐ 53 Fossgate ❶ 01904 654904

The Golden Fleece ⑳ Reputed to be the city's most haunted inn with a multitude of apparitions from various periods of its long 500-year history said to leave their mark on guests. Some good beer, open-mike nights and twice-monthly comedy clubs should help distract nervous customers. ⓐ 16 Pavement ❶ 01904 625171 ⓦ www.goldenfleece.yorkwebsites.co.uk

Kings Arms ㉑ Historic and traditional pub on the banks of the river, made famous for the number of times it gets submerged during exceptional high tides. Its location, terrace (river permitting) and fame make it extremely busy and noisy over holiday weekends (see feature box opposite). ⓐ 3 King's Staith ❶ 01904 659435

KINGS ARMS

This former 17th-century customs house, now a pub commemorating Richard III (see opposite) on the banks of the River Ouse, is infamous for its tendency to flood each year when the river reaches higher than normal levels and breaches its banks. So regularly does this happen that anything prone to water damage is kept high off the ground; furniture is on hinges, or can be removed completely, while the beer barrels are kept upstairs as opposed to in the traditional cellar. The staff are also well versed in flood damage limitation and can clear the building in an hour. These acts of nature are now celebrated in photographs within, as well as with a plaque for measuring water levels.

◆ *Enjoying a fine spring day in the Museum Gardens*

RESTAURANTS

Fiesta Mehicana £ ② Lively and popular Mexican restaurant serving long-established favourites alongside one or two less authentic dishes for the gringos. They also offer a gluten-free and skinny menu. It has a colourfully bright fiesta atmosphere. ⓐ 14 Clifford Street ⓣ 01904 610243 ⓦ www.fiestamehicana.com ⓛ 17.30–23.00 daily

Russells £ ② No-nonsense, unpretentious cooking in this traditional, affordable and popular British carvery. The choices of roasted meats at the buffet table are the big draw here, but à la carte options and choices for vegetarians are also available. The desserts menu includes English favourites such as homemade bread and butter pudding and treacle sponge. ⓐ 26 Coppergate ⓣ 01904 644330 ⓦ www.russells-restaurants.com ⓛ 12.00–21.30 Mon–Sat, 12.00–17.00 Sun

Blue Bicycle ££ ② Rumoured to have been dedicated to pleasures of the flesh in the past (see page 68), this highly regarded Mediterranean bistro specialising in seafood now offers good dining in its shabby chic interior. ⓐ 34 Fossgate ⓣ 01904 673990 ⓦ www.thebluebicycle.com ⓛ 18.00–21.30 Mon–Wed, 12.00–14.30 & 18.00–21.30 Thur–Sat, 12.00–14.30 & 18.00–21.00 Sun

J Bakers ££ ② Excellent British food with inspiring twists on old favourites served in a low-key and informal bistro atmosphere. 'Grazing menus' are available to get a fuller experience boldly creative yet ultimately comforting dishes on offer. For some pure

sweet indulgence, visit their chocolate room upstairs.
ⓐ 7 Fossgate ⓣ 01904 622688 ⓦ www.jbakers.co.uk ⓛ 12.00–
14.30 & 18.00–22.00 daily

Melton's Too ££ ㉖ Another fine Walmgate eatery housed in a 17th-century building atop a cosy and popular bar. This casual and

△ *The neoclassical Castle Museum*

friendly bistro is a celebration of both local and international produce, serving innovative local favourites alongside specialities from the Mediterranean, including tapas and meze dishes.
ⓐ 25 Walmgate ⓣ 01904 629222 ⓦ www.meltonstoo.co.uk
ⓛ 10.30–24.00 Mon–Sat, 10.30–23.00 Sun

THEATRE

Grand Opera House ㉗ A regular venue for big-name stars of comedy and music, along with touring West End hits and children's shows. ⓐ Clifford Street ⓣ 0844 847 2322
ⓦ www.grandoperahouseyork.org.uk ⓛ Box office: 12.00–17.30 Mon–Sat

FOSSGATE & WALMGATE

Quite underwhelming at first glance, these two conjoined streets have long been linked with food and eating and are now the centre of York's dining scene. Fossgate (named after the Foss River it bridges) was for a long time host of the local sea fish market, which was opened by the ringing of the 'Scatybell' at nearby St Mary's Church. It also earned itself quite a reputation for shady dealings, and was for a while known locally as 'Tricksters' Lane'. Walmgate too was tarred with a similar brush, earning a reputation for drink and debauchery during the Victorian period, when it was said to have more pubs than houses. During demolition work in the 1960s, mysterious tunnels were found under Fossgate, which are thought to be part of the Roman sewer system.

Outside the city centre

This is a large area that encircles the city walls, stretching to a radius of around 50 km (30 miles). Some of the listings below can be reached on foot in little more than 20 minutes from the Minster, while if heading out beyond the city boundaries you will require bus or car transport (see page 37).

SIGHTS & ATTRACTIONS

Cold War Bunker
One of the more unusual attractions of the city, this is a fascinating, somewhat disturbing site. In service from the 1960s, the blast-proof doors open up to a collection of operational rooms built as a nerve centre in the event of a genuinely feared nuclear war. An introductory film is followed by one-hour guided tours. ⓐ Monument Close, Acomb Road ⓣ 01904 646940 (shared number with Clifford's Tower) ⓦ www.english-heritage.org.uk ⓛ Sat & Sun 1st and 3rd weekends of the month plus bank holidays ⓘ Admission charge. Limited parking

Flamingo Land
Large theme park and zoo with strong conservation credentials offering fun, education and plenty of thrilling and dizzying rides for all ages, accompanied by feature shows, events and choice of places to grab a bite (see map page 84). ⓐ Kirby Misperton, Malton ⓣ 0871 911 8000 ⓦ www.flamingoland.co.uk ⓛ 10.00–17.00 daily, Mar–Oct Ⓝ Bus: 840 ⓘ Admission charge

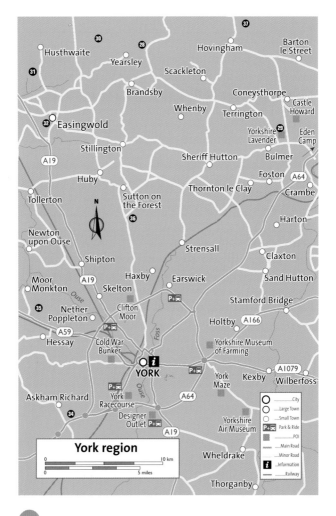

York region

York Maze

The largest maize maze in the world and a chance to lose oneself for a spell. Clues and viewing towers help participants along the way, plus there are plenty of other activities beyond the giant corn labyrinth. ⓐ Elvington Lane ⓣ 01904 607341 ⓦ www.yorkmaze.com ⓛ 10.00–16.30 daily July–Sept ⓘ Admission charge

CULTURE

Castle Howard

Made famous as the principal location for the classic TV adaptation of *Brideshead Revisited*, this magnificent and still occupied 18th-century residence, complete with long gallery and chapel, is one of the jewels in the UK's heritage and cultural crown. Surrounding the sumptuous Howard family home are formal gardens, parklands, temples and water features along with a nursery and selection of shops and cafés in the former carriage buildings. There's also an adventure playground for children. ⓐ Castle Howard ⓣ 01653 648444 ⓦ www.castlehoward.co.uk ⓛ The house: 11.00–16.00 daily Mar–Oct & late Nov–Dec; gardens 10.00–18.30 (dusk in winter) ⓝ Train: Malton, then either taxi (**Station Taxis** ⓐ 18 Church Street, Malton ⓣ 01653 696969 ⓘ approx £15) or Bus: 183 from outside the station ⓘ Admission charge

Eden Camp

Multi-award-winning, engaging museum housed in the original barracks of a Second World War prisoner-of-war camp. Covering almost every aspect of the 1939–45 war, it could certainly take half a day to explore. Excellent value, and has two assault courses on which livelier visitors can burn off energy as well as the Prisoner's Canteen and Officer's Mess offering hot meals and snacks. ⓐ Malton ⓣ 01653 697777 ⓦ www.edencamp.co.uk ⓛ 10.00–16.00 daily, closed Christmas and New Year ⓝ Bus: 840 ⓘ Admission charge

Yorkshire Air Museum

Wonderfully engaging aviation museum based on a historic Bomber Command station. Many of the original buildings –

⬥ Castle Howard and its beautiful grounds

including hangars, mess huts and the control tower – are employed as display rooms, which all adds to the atmosphere. ⓐ Halifax Road, Elvington ① 01904 608595 ⓦ www.yorkshireairmuseum.co.uk ⏰ 10.00–17.00 daily (summer); 10.00–15.30 daily (winter) ⓘ Admission charge

Yorkshire Museum of Farming

Animals and local agricultural history, and a creative explanation of the farming season, make this a great destination for all ages. Children are particularly well looked after, and with a miniature railway, Roman fort, Viking village and a series of special events throughout the year this is a winner. ⓐ Murton Park, Murton Lane ① 01904 489966 ⓦ www.murtonpark.co.uk ⏰ 10.00–17.00 daily (summer); 10.00–16.00 daily (winter) ⓘ Admission charge

RETAIL THERAPY

Apart from a selection of independent shops lining Gillygate, there is not much shopping to be had in the streets immediately outside the city walls; however, all the attractions listed do come with gift shops as part of the visiting experience. A popular tourist destination in its own right is the **York Designer Outlet**, which offers 115 discounted designer and high street stores in enclosed comfort. There is also a large food hall offering self- and full-service restaurants. ⓐ St Nicholas Avenue, Fulford ① 01904 682700 ⓦ www.yorkdesigneroutlet.com ⏰ 10.00–18.00 Mon–Sat, 10.00–20.00 Thur, 11.00–17.00 Sun ⓝ Bus: 7

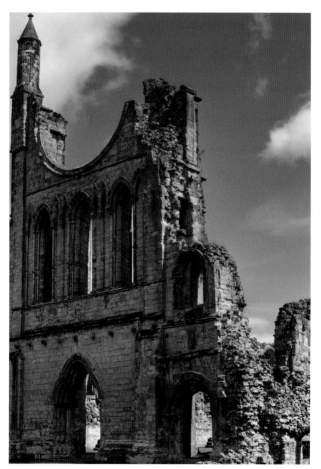

⬭ *The ruins of Byland Abbey, across the road from The Abbey Inn*

TAKING A BREAK

CAFÉS

Ampleforth Abbey Tea Room £ ㉘ Housed within the thriving Benedictine community of Ampleforth Abbey, this is a charming place fitted out with furniture made by popular local craftsman 'Mousey' Thompson. Indulge in some wonderful homemade desserts and light snacks. ⓐ Ampleforth Abbey, Ampleforth ⓣ 01439 766000 ⓦ www.hpo.ampleforth.org.uk ⓛ 10.00–17.30 Mon–Sat, 12.00–17.30 Sun

EJ's £ ㉙ Bright and airy tea room at the heart of the Yorkshire Lavender Farm and Gardens, serving a fine menu of light snacks including lavender-flavoured scones and ice creams. ⓐ Terrington ⓣ 01653 648008 ⓦ www.yorkshirelavender.com ⓛ 10.00–17.00 daily

PUBS & BARS

The Abbey Inn ㉚ Charming, isolated pub, built from the stones used to construct the now ruined Byland Abbey across the road. Local real ales and guest beers, along with elegant, simple food, are served with some flair in the cosy bar rooms, making this a popular stopping-off point for history enthusiasts, tourists and the wedding parties that employ the romantic abbey setting. ⓐ Byland Abbey ⓣ 01347 868204 ⓦ www.theappletree.org ⓛ Wed–Mon, closed Tues

Fauconberg Arms ㉛ Located in the award-winning and idyllic village of Coxwold, this family run 17th-century country inn ticks all the boxes for a great pub experience: real ales, real fires and genuine hospitality. Enjoy some hearty English food or join in one of the monthly Monday pub quizzes. ❸ Main Street, Coxwold ❶ 01347 868214 Ⓦ www.fauconbergarms.com

The George ❸❷ Convivial pub for locals and visitors set in the heart of bustling and picturesque Easingwold. Overlooking the cobbled historic square, this former 18th-century coaching inn is

⬥ *Learn about Yorkshire's sheep at the Museum of Farming*

all oak beams, brasses, nooks and corners; the menu offers traditional food in generous portions. ⓐ Market Place, Easingwold ⓣ 01347 821698 ⓦ www.the-george-hotel.co.uk

Masons Arms ㉝ Just beyond the city wall, and fairly unremarkable from the front, this Free House mock-Tudor pub is home to some genuine historical features inside, and has a rear beer garden with lovely views over the River Foss. ⓐ 6 Fishergate ⓣ 01904 646046 ⓦ www.masonsarmsyork.co.uk

RESTAURANTS

Tritons £ ㉞ Although business-like in appearance, this large, open-plan restaurant offers some of the best fish and chips to be found in the area. Along with a choice of family favourites – lasagne, burgers, giant Yorkshire Puddings and the like – there are also some rather good desserts. Gluten-free dishes are also available, as is takeaway. ⓐ Bilbrough Top, Tadcaster Road ⓣ 01904 700189 ⓦ www.tritonsfishandchips.co.uk

The Alice Hawthorn ££ ㉟ A beautiful village green setting, with duck pond and highland cattle nearby, form a backdrop to this traditional historic inn. It serves a choice of classic pub favourites or innovative à la carte in its friendly and charmingly decorated bar and restaurants. ⓐ Nun Monkton ⓣ 01423 330303 ⓦ www.the-alice.co.uk

The Rose and Crown ££ ㊱ Michelin- and AA-commended, gourmands will find plenty to delight on a menu that uses locally caught fish, seafood and Yorkshire-reared meat. The

atmosphere is warm and hospitable, with the décor a mixture of rustic and refined. Early bird specials are available.
ⓐ Main Street, Sutton on the Forest ① 01347 811333
Ⓦ www.rosecrown.co.uk ● 12.00–14.00 Tues–Sun, 18.00–21.00 Mon–Sat

The Star Inn ££–£££ ㊲ Much-lauded restaurant housed in a former 14th-century thatched longhouse. Impeccably friendly staff serve creative and pioneering dishes, 95 per cent of which are sourced from its own garden or the surrounding countryside. A chef's table is available for groups of up to eight; you can take a tour of the kitchen garden and help the chef as your eight-course meal is prepared. Booking for the restaurant is strongly recommended. ⓐ High Street, Harome ① 01439 770397
Ⓦ www.thestaratharome.co.uk ● 11.30–14.00, 18.30–21.30 Tues–Sat, 12.00–18.00 Sun, 18.30–21.30 Mon

● A stream in the heart of the Dales

OUT OF TOWN
trips

North York Moors

Wild and ravishing in equal measure, these landscapes combine heather-draped moors, rich pasture, ancient forests and dramatic coastline. The stunning backdrop is sprinkled with alluring towns and villages, all joined by narrow country lanes that beg to be explored. For more information the National Park Authority (☎ 01439 770657 ⓦ www.northyorkmoors.org.uk) has visitor centres in Danby, Sutton Bank, Helmsley and Robin Hood's Bay.

GETTING THERE

Travelling by road takes around an hour from the centre of York, with the A169 the major route through the national park. By public transport, The Yorkshire **Coastliner** bus (☎ 01653 692556 ⓦ www.yorkbus.co.uk Ⓝ Bus: 840, X40) picks up at York Station and continues on through the Dales, stopping at a number of villages before terminating in Whitby. The **Moorsbus** (☎ 01845 597000 ⓦ www.northyorkmoors.org.uk) connects many of the villages to the towns of Thirsk, Helmsley and Pickering. For train services, see under North Yorkshire Moors Railway below.

SIGHTS & ATTRACTIONS

North Yorkshire Moors Railway
Enjoy a steam journey between Pickering and Whitby, stopping at charmingly restored rural stations. Goathland is the celebrity

standout as both the station location for 'Hogsmeade' in the first Harry Potter film and as Aidensfield in TV's *Heartbeat*.

ⓐ 2 Park Street, Pickering ⓣ 01751 472508 ⓦ www.nymr.co.uk
ⓛ Daily (spring & summer) ⓝ Bus: 840 to Pickering or Whitby
ⓘ Charge for travel only

Village tour

A car or bus tour through some of the beautiful villages in the area is a wonderful way to spend some time. Hutton Le Hole, Helmsley, Goathland, Great Ayton, Danby and Robin Hood's Bay are just some of the ancient communities worth a visit (for bus information, see above).

World of James Herriot

The former veterinary practice belonging to the author of the world-famous vet books has been restored to show how it would have looked in the 1940s when Alf Wight (aka James Herriot) worked there. There are also interactive and fun exhibits from the TV series based on his life and work.

ⓐ 23 Kirkgate, Thirsk ⓣ 01845 525333
ⓦ www.worldofjamesherriot.org ⓛ 10.00–16.00 daily (summer); 11.00–15.00 daily (winter) ⓘ Admission charge

CULTURE

Rievaulx Abbey

One of the best-preserved abbeys in Britain, this soaring, 900-year-old edifice is hidden in the tranquil Rye Valley. A tour around the atmospheric ruins is enhanced by audio guides

relating tales of monastic life.  Helmsley ⓣ 01439 798228
ⓦ www.english-heritage.org.uk ⓛ 10.00–18.00 daily (Apr–Sept);
10.00–16.00 Thur–Mon (Oct–Mar) ⓝ Bus: Moorsbus M8, M91
ⓘ Admission charge

Ryedale Folk Museum

Set in the gorgeous village of Hutton-le-Hole, this outdoor
museum covers all aspects of rural life through the ages in a
series of recreated Ryedale buildings. ⓐ Hutton-le-Hole
ⓣ 01751 417367 ⓦ www.ryedalefolkmuseum.co.uk ⓛ 10.00–16.30
(summer); 10.00–dusk (winter) ⓝ Bus: Moorsbus M3
ⓘ Admission charge

RETAIL THERAPY

The market towns of Thirsk (ⓦ www.visit-thirsk.com), Pickering
(ⓦ www.pickering.uk.net) and Helmsley (ⓦ www.ryedale.co.uk),
all come with a fine selection of weekly markets (Thirsk:
Monday & Saturday; Pickering: Monday; Helmsley: Friday).

TAKING A BREAK

The Barn Tea Rooms £ Overlooking beautiful village greenery
and stone houses, this quaint tea room offers a selection of light
snacks, including afternoon tea, along with filling hot meals.
ⓐ Hutton-le-Hole ⓣ 01751 417311 ⓦ www.thebarnhotel.info

Goathland Hotel £ Busy traditional 'brasses and beams' pub in
the heart of the village, made famous for its role as the

'Aidensfield Arms' in TV's *Heartbeat*. Standard hearty pub food is served through the day and into the early evening. ⓐ Goathland ⓣ 01947 896203 ⓦ www.goathlandhotel.co.uk

Station buffets £ For rail enthusiasts and those planning a journey on the North Yorkshire Moors steam railway, the stations at Pickering, Goathland and Grossmont all have heritage tea rooms (see page 80). ⓣ 01751 472508 ⓦ www.nymr.co.uk

The Anvil Inn ££ On the southern boundaries of the moors, this former 18th-century forge now prides itself on its regionally sourced produce to create a British- and Mediterranean-influenced menu. Bookings strongly recommended. ⓐ Main Street, Sawdon ⓣ 01723 859896 ⓦ www.theanvilinnsawdon.co.uk

▲ *Goathland Station*

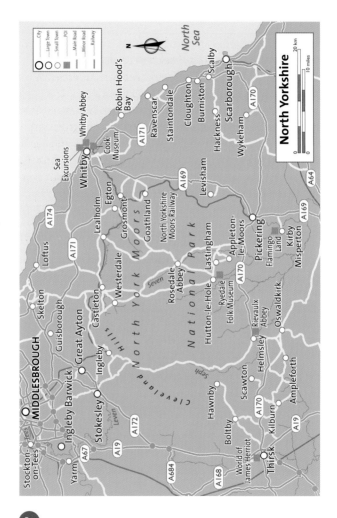

North Yorkshire

Whitby

Dominated by the brooding abbey high above, Whitby is a wonderful, gorge-sided seaside resort and harbour, each half having a separate and distinct personality. The west side is home to the **tourist office** (ⓐ Langbourne Road ☎ 01723 383636 ⓦ www.discoveryorkshirecoast.com ⏰ 09.00–21.00 (summer); 09.00–18.00 (winter)) and the bulk of the accommodation, as well as the sandy beach, boat excursions and penny slot arcades. The east is home to the winding narrow streets of the old town, Whitby Abbey and an eclectic range of shops.

GETTING THERE

Travelling to Whitby by road from York can be a lovely experience, as the main A169 passes amongst the stunning North York Moors scenery; however, on arrival during peak holiday times and weekends, parking in or even close to the town can be troublesome. As an alternative, hop aboard one of the Coastliner buses (see page 80) for the journey from York Station, which takes just over two hours. Alternatively, take the same, shorter service to Pickering to catch the heritage railway from there to Whitby (see pages 80–81).

SIGHTS & ATTRACTIONS

Cook Museum
Former lodgings of epic explorer and cartographer Captain Cook. This 17th-century building has four floors dedicated to

celebrating the maritime career of Yorkshire-born James Cook.
ⓐ Grape Lane ⓣ 01947 601900
ⓦ www.cookmuseumwhitby.co.uk ⓛ 09.45–16.00 daily (Apr–Oct); 11.00–14.30 daily (Mar only)

Sea excursions

There are a host of companies along the western harbour walls offering short trips out of the harbour into the North Sea. The *Endeavour* is one such ship, a scaled-down replica of Captain Cook's famous discovery vessel (ⓣ 01723 364100

⬥ *Goths and tall ships in Whitby*

GO GOTH

Published in 1897, a large proportion of Bram Stoker's much-filmed novel *Dracula* is set in Whitby. Since then, the town has become synonymous with Gothic culture, which is stronger today than it's ever been. Numerous shops sell all kinds of Goth-and-gore clothing and accessories. But it's not all black and gloomy shoe gazing. The highlight is the twice-yearly, April and October Goth festivals, attracting all ages to come together and dress in some authentically beautiful Victorian and Edwardian costumes (Ⓦ www.whitbygothicfestival.co.uk).

Ⓦ www.endeavourwhitby.com). Alternatively, *Esk Belle II* (Ⓣ 07941 450381 Ⓦ www.whitbycoastalcruises.co.uk) is a bigger boat complete with bar.

Whitby Abbey

Originally founded in 657, the abbey has had a long and turbulent past, the older building long since destroyed. This Gothic building, begun in about 1220, was a Benedictine abbey, pillaged by Henry VIII and later shelled by the German Navy. Today its ruins stand high above the town and crashing sea below. The climb from the Old Town up the 199 steps is worth it for the views alone, though it can be circuitously accessed by car. ⓐ Abbey Lane Ⓣ 01947 603568 Ⓦ www.english-heritage.org.uk Ⓛ 10.00–18.00 daily (summer); 10.00–16.00 Thur–Mon (winter) ⓘ Admission charge

TAKING A BREAK

Abbey Steps £ Small and charming tea room in the Old Town that serves light bites, including locally caught crab sandwiches. It makes an excellent rest stop on the way up or down to the abbey and also offers bed & breakfast accommodation. ⓐ 117 Church Street ⓣ 01947 601271 ⓦ www.abbeystepsbandb.co.uk

Duke of York £ This quaint and intimate 'olde worlde' pub on a maritime theme is at the far end of the old town and offers a warm atmosphere, hearty fare and some wonderful views across the harbour and out to the North Sea. ⓐ Church Street ⓦ www.dukeofyork.co.uk ⓣ 01947 600324

Moon and Sixpence ££ Stylish, relaxed bar and bistro, specialising in seafood and offering grand views of the harbour and live piano music. Booking recommended. ⓐ Marine Parade ⓣ 01947 604416 ⓦ www.moon-and-sixpence.co.uk ⓛ 10.00–24.00 daily

● *Bristling signposts pointing the way*

PRACTICAL
information

Directory

GETTING THERE

By air

Leeds/Bradford Airport (☎ 0871 288 2288
ⓦ www.leedsbradfordairport.co.uk) is about 45 minutes by car
from the centre of York and is served by budget airlines such as
Jet2 (ⓦ www.jet2.com), Ryanair (ⓦ www.ryanair.com) and Flybe
(ⓦ www.flybe.com). The nearest major airport is at **Manchester**
(☎ 0871 271 0711 ⓦ www.manchesterairport.co.uk).

Also nearby are **Durham Tees Valley Airport** (☎ 0871 224 2426
ⓦ www.durhamteesvalleyairport.com) and **Robin Hood Airport
Doncaster Sheffield** (☎ 0871 220 2210
ⓦ www.robinhoodairport.com).

Many people are aware that air travel emits CO_2,
which contributes to climate change. You may be interested
in the possibility of lessening the environmental impact
of your flight through the charity **Climate Care**
(ⓦ www.jpmorganclimatecare.com), which offsets your CO_2
by funding environmental projects around the world.

By rail

There are regular services to London (2 hours) and Edinburgh
(2½ hours). Contact **National Rail** for details (☎ 0845 748 4950
ⓦ www.nationalrail.co.uk).

By road

There are no direct motorways to York, though the A1 London to
Newcastle route does get fairly close. From there either the A64 or

A59 lead to the outer ring road (A1237 and A64) circling the city, from which a number of smaller and often traffic-heavy spur roads lead to its heart. **National Express** coaches have regular services from London's Victoria Coach Station to York Railway Station in 5 hours 15 minutes, on average (☎ 0871 781 8178 ⓦ www.nationalexpress.com). Alternatively **Megabus** offers extremely cheap coach travel from London to York, dropping passengers off just outside the city centre (ⓦ www.megabus.com).

By ferry

York is only a short road and rail journey from the port of Hull on the east coast; from there, crossings to mainland Europe are served by **P&O Ferries** (☎ 0871 664 5645 ⓦ www.poferries.com). Visitors from Northern Ireland travelling via Liverpool should contact **Norfolk Line** (☎ 0844 847 5042 ⓦ www.norfolkline.com).

HEALTH, SAFETY & CRIME

Like many popular destinations York attracts pickpockets to crowded areas, so it is wise to keep money, cameras and phones tucked away. Shield ATMs from prying eyes and don't let inebriated companions go wandering off alone. Take your hotel's business card before a night out to show to taxi drivers in case you get lost. Finally, for overseas visitors, water from taps is fine to drink.

Emergency contacts

If you require **police**, **fire brigade** or **ambulance**, call ☎ 999. For non-emergencies call **North Yorkshire Police** ☎ 0845 606 0247 or see ⓦ www.northyorkshire.police.uk

Late-night pharmacy
Boots ⓐ Unit 7 Monks Cross Shopping Park ⓣ 01904 656360
ⓛ 09.00–24.00 Mon–Sat, 11.00–17.00 Sun

Medical advice
The **NHS Walk-In Centre** offers nurse-led treatment for minor
illnesses and injuries without appointment. ⓐ 31 Monkgate
ⓣ 01904 725401 ⓛ 08.00–18.00 daily.
York Hospital is a 15-minute walk from the city centre and
includes an accident and emergency department.
ⓐ Wigginton Road ⓣ 01904 631313 ⓦ www.york.nhs.uk
ⓝ Bus: 6
For medical advice, contact **NHS Direct** for 24-hour telephone
information. (ⓣ 0845 46 47 ⓦ www.nhsdirect.nhs.uk).

Dentists
For out-of-hours advice, NHS-registered patients should contact
the **NHS Dental Helpline** (ⓣ 0845 600 3249 ⓛ 18.00–06.00
daily) or visit ⓦ www.nhs.uk for a list of York practices. For non-
registered NHS patients needing emergency treatment during
normal office hours ⓣ 01904 725 422.

OPENING HOURS
Most of York's shops open between 09.00 or 10.00 and 17.30,
Monday to Saturday, and between 11.00 and 16.00 on Sundays
(smaller convenience stores are generally open for longer). Most
shops and attractions will also be open on bank holidays, except
Christmas Day and Easter Sunday. Banks are open between
09.30 and 16.30 Monday to Friday, many also on Saturday

mornings. They are closed on bank holidays. ATMs are widely available for free cash withdrawals.

TOILETS

The most central public convenience – on Silver Street – charges 30 pence. Free toilets can be found, however, at Castlegate (overlooking the car park), at the corner of St Leonard's Place and Petergate and at the Nunnery Lane car park.

CHILDREN

Attractions such as Jorvik and the Castle Museum have gone to great lengths to make history entertaining for all age groups. Teenagers will probably enjoy the York Dungeon. Flamingo Land (see page 69) is a good choice for youngsters, and Whitby offers all kinds of traditional seaside attractions for children.

TRAVELLERS WITH DISABILITIES

The **Shopmobility** scheme offers rental services for equipment including wheelchairs and scooters. ⓐ Level 2, Piccadilly Car Park ⓣ 01904 679222 ⓦ www.shopmobilityyork.org.uk ⓛ 10.00–16.00 Mon–Sat (Apr–Oct); 10.00–16.00 Tues–Sat (Nov–Mar), closed bank holidays ⓝ Bus: 10, 24, 8P&R (yellow route)

FURTHER INFORMATION

York Visitor Centre ⓐ 1 Museum Street ⓣ 01904 550099 ⓦ www.visityork.org ⓛ 09.00–17.00 (18.00 in summer) Mon–Sat; 10.00–16.00 (17.00 in summer) Sun ⓝ Bus: 1, 5, 6 Another very useful website is: ⓦ www.yorkshire.com

ACKNOWLEDGEMENTS

The photographs in this book were taken by Joni Audas for Thomas Cook Publishing, to whom the copyright belongs, except for the following: Dreamstime page 74 (Kevin Eaves); iStockphoto page 72 (Greg Panosian), 79 (pollyconn), 83 (GB Photostock); Shutterstock page 76 (Diane Webb).

Project editor: Thomas Willsher
Copy editor: Penny Isaac
Proofreaders: Edmund French & Beth Beemer
Layout: Trevor Double
Indexer: Penelope Kent

AUTHOR BIOGRAPHY

A member of the British Guild of Travel Writers, and published throughout the world, freelance travel writer and broadcaster David Cawley is a card-carrying northerner specialising in UK & European destinations. A regular visitor to the city professionally and during his 'down-time', David is a mammoth champion of York and its surroundings.

Send your thoughts to
books@thomascook.com

- Found a great bar, club, shop or must-see sight that we don't feature?

- Like to tip us off about any information that needs a little updating?

- Want to tell us what you love about this handy little guidebook and more importantly how we can make it even handier?

Then here's your chance to tell all! Send us ideas, discoveries and recommendations today and then look out for your valuable input in the next edition of this title.

Email the above address (stating the title) or write to:
pocket guides Series Editor, Thomas Cook Publishing, PO Box 227, Coningsby Road, Peterborough PE3 8SB, UK.